OUR WORLD 1

T0288509

s Editors
Kang Shin
) Crandall

SECOND EDITION • GRAMMAR WORKBOOK

NATIONAL GEOGRAPHIC LEARNING

Australia • Brazil • Mexico • Singapore • United Kingdom • United States

Unit 1

Yes/No* questions with *it's

Question				Answer		
Is	**it**	an	eraser?	Yes, **it is.**	**It's** an eraser.	*It's = It is*
		a	pen?	No, **it isn't.**	**It's** a crayon.	*isn't = is not*

***Is it** a clock? No, **it isn't**. **It's** a map.*

1 **Unscramble.** Write a question.

1. c c k o l ______clock______ ______Is it a clock______?
2. p a m ____________ ____________?
3. n l c p e i ____________ ____________?
4. n e p ____________ ____________?

2 **Look and read.** Write the answer.

1.  Is it a clock? ______Yes, it is______.
2.  Is it a crayon? ____________.
3. 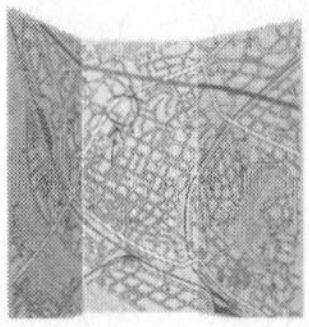 Is it a map? ____________.
4.  Is it a board? ____________.

3 **Write.** Look at Activity 2.

1. It's a clock.
2. ______________________.
3. ______________________.
4. ______________________.

4 **Look and write.**

1.  It's a circle.
2.  ______________________.
3.  ______________________.
4.  ______________________.

5 **Draw and write.** Draw a picture of your classroom. Write 2 questions and 2 answers.

____

____

____

____

What* and *How many

Question				Answer
What		is	it?	It's an eraser.
	color	is	it?	It's orange.

Question	Answer
How many erasers?	Three.

What asks about a thing. *How many* asks for a number.

1 **Read and match.** Draw a line.

1. Is it a — a. it?
2. It's an — b. picture?
3. What color — c. is it?
4. What is — d. papers?
5. How many — e. eraser.

2 **Read.** Write *What*, *What's*, or *How*.

1. ______________ your name? I'm Sandy.
2. ______________ color is it? It's purple.
3. ______________ many pictures? Six.
4. ______________ is it? It's a chair.

3 **Read and write.** Complete the questions.

1. ______What is it______? It's a book.
2. ____________________? It's black.
3. ____________________ chairs? Five.

4 Look and write.

1. 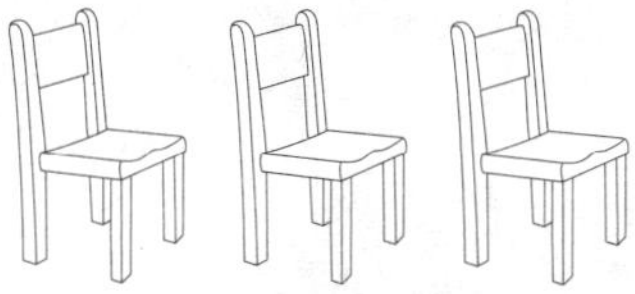

How many chairs ________?

Three ________.

2. 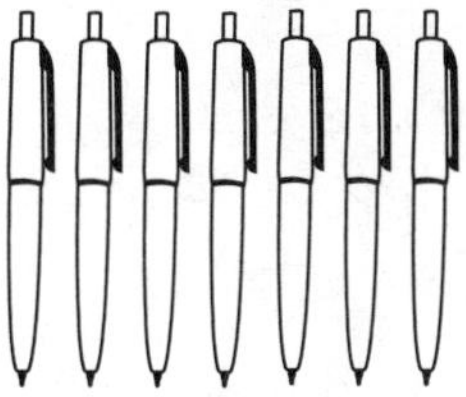

________________?

________.

3. 

________________?

________.

4. 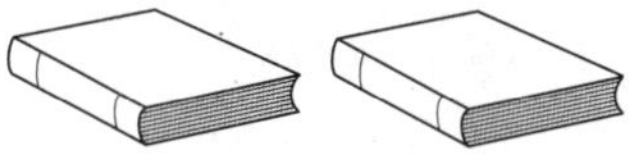

________________?

________.

5 **Write.** Color the picture. Answer the questions.

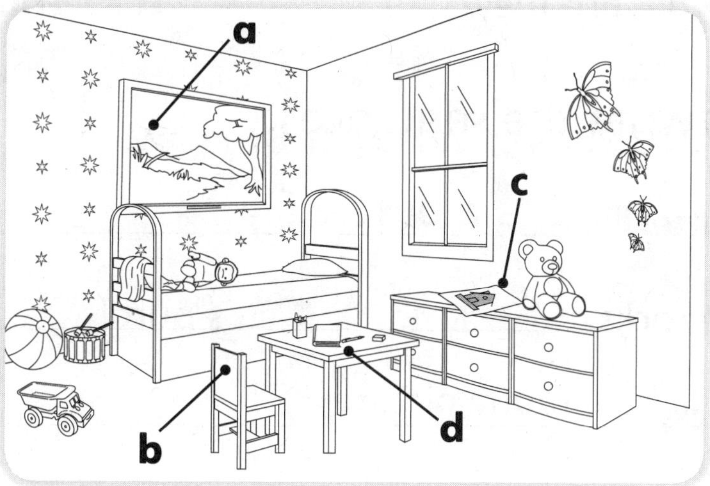

1. Look at **a**. What is it?

________.

2. Look at **b**. What color is it?

________.

3. Look at **c**. What is it?

________.

4. Look at **d**. What color is it?

________.

Unit 2

to be: is, are

Question			Answer		
What	**is**	it?	**It's**	a tree.	*It's = It is*
	are	they?	**They're**	trees.	*They're = They are*

one thing = ***It's*** *a flower.*

two or more things = ***They're*** *flowers.*

1 Read. Circle the words.

1. **What / Is** it a river? — Yes, it **is / are**.
2. What **is / are** it? — It **'s / are** a bird.
3. What **is / are** they? — They **is / are** frogs.
4. **What / How** are they? — **It's / They're** rocks.

2 Read. Rewrite the sentences.

1. It is a butterfly. It's a butterfly.
2. They are rocks. ______________.
3. It is a stick. ______________.
4. They are trees. ______________.

3 **Look.** Write questions.

1. What is it ?
2. ________________?
3. ________________?
4. ________________?
5. ________________?

4 **Look.** Answer the questions in Activity 3. Use the picture.

1. It's a mountain .
2. ________________.
3. ________________.
4. ________________.
5. ________________.

5 **Look and write.** Write 2 questions and 2 answers about the picture in Activity 2.

________________? ________________?

________________. ________________.

Where* and *in* or *on

Question			Answer
Where	is	the moon?	It's **in** the sky.
	are	the birds?	They're **on** the rock.

Use *in* or *on* + a place: ***in*** the tree, ***on*** the grass

1 Read. Circle the letter.

1. The clouds are ________ the sky. a. is b. on c. in
2. The trees ________ in the grass. a. is b. are c. on
3. The rainbow ________ in the sky. a. is b. on c. are
4. Where ________ the parrots? a. is b. in c. are
5. The monkey is ________ the rock. a. in b. are c. on

2 Look. Write *in* or *on*.

1. The bird is _____ the tree.
2. The rocks are _____ the river.
3. The star is _____ the sky.
4. The bird is _____ the stick.

3 Look and write.

1.  Where is the butterfly?

2.  ____________________?

3.  ____________________?

4.  ____________________?

4 **Write.** Answer the questions in Activity 3.

1. It's on the grass.
2. ____________________.
3. ____________________.
4. ____________________.

5 **Look and write.** Look outside. Write 3 questions and answers about what you see.

Where's the sun? It's in the sky.

____

____

____

Unit 3

to have

Question	Answer			
How many sisters do you have?	I	**have**	one sister.	*don't = do not*
		don't have	any sisters.	

*I **have** one baby sister/two big brothers.*

*I **don't have** any brothers.*

1 **Write.** Unscramble the sentences.

1. brother / have / a / I / big

   I have a big brother.

2. have / sister / a / I / baby

   ________________.

3. a / don't / brother / I / have

   ________________.

4. parents / I / two / have

   ________________.

2 **Read and write.** Give answers that are true for you.

1. Do you have any sisters?

   ________________.

2. How many parents ________________?

   ________________.

3. How many grandfathers ________________?

   ________________.

4. ________________ any brothers?

   ________________.

3 Look and write.

1. sister I don't have any sisters ____________.
2. mother ____________.
3. father ____________.
4. brother ____________.
5. grandfather ____________.

4 **Write.** Write questions to ask a friend about family. Use the words in the box.

(baby/big) brother	(baby/big) sister	grandfather/grandmother

1. Do you have a baby sister ____________?
2. ____________?
3. ____________?
4. ____________?

5 **Write.** Write 2 sentences about your family. Use *have*.

____

____

He/She and questions with *who*

Question		Answer	*Who's = Who is*
Who's	**he**?	**He's** my brother Jack.	*He's = He is*
	she?	**She's** my sister Ana.	*She's = She is*

Who asks about a person.

he = a boy/man   *she* = a girl/woman

1 Look and write.

1. Who's he?
2. ______________
3. ______________

2 Look and write. Imagine this is your family.

1. Who's he? He's my baby brother. He's two.

2. Who's she? ______________________. She's short.

3. Who's he? ______________________. He's old.

4. Who's she? ______________________. She's tall.

3 **Write.** Write questions and answers.

1. Who's he ____________________?

He's my big brother. He's tall ____________________. (tall)

2. ____________________?

____________________. (young)

3. ____________________?

____________________. (ten)

4. ____________________?

____________________. (small)

4 **Draw and write.** Draw 2 people in your family. Then write about them. Use the words in the box.

old	short	tall	young

____

____

____

____

Review: Units 1–3

1 **Read and match.** Draw a line.

1. Who's he?
2. Where is the bird?
3. What are they?
4. What color is it?
5. What is it?
6. Is it a bird?
7. How many books?

a. Three.
b. It's in the sky.
c. He's my grandfather.
d. They're birds.
e. It's a bird.
f. No, it isn't. It's a frog.
g. It's blue.

2 **Look and write.** Complete the questions.

1. ____________ a book?
2. What color ____________?
3. ____________ she?
4. What ____________?
5. ____________ the tree?
6. How many brothers ____________?

3 **Write.** Answer the questions in Activity 2.

1. ______________________.
2. ______________________.
3. ______________________.
4. ______________________.
5. ______________________.
6. ______________________.

4 **Look and write.**

1. 

The birds ______________________.

2. 

______________________ the grass.

3. 

______________________.

4. 

______________________.

5 **Look and color.** Write sentences.

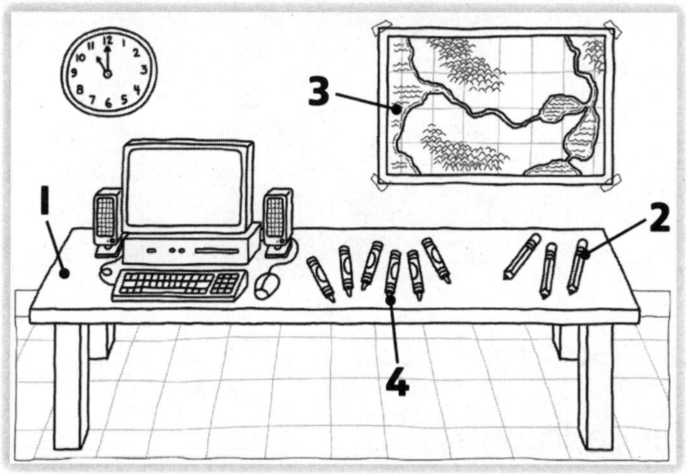

1. It's yellow ______________________.
2. ______________________.
3. ______________________.
4. ______________________.

Unit 4

Yes/No* questions with *Is there . . . ?

Question			Answer	
Is there	a lamp	in the bedroom?	Yes, **there is**.	*isn't = is not*
	a TV	in the kitchen?	No, **there isn't**.	

Is there *a mirror in the kitchen? No,* ***there isn't****.*

1 **Read.** Look at your house. Circle the letter.

1. Is there a sofa in the bedroom?

   a. Yes, there is. b. No, there isn't.

2. Is there a clock in the kitchen?

   a. Yes, there is. b. No, there isn't.

3. Is there a chair in the living room?

   a. Yes, there is. b. No, there isn't.

4. Is there a lamp in the dining room?

   a. Yes, there is. b. No, there isn't.

2 **Look and write.**

1. Is there a sofa in the bedroom? No, there isn't.
2. ______ a lamp in the bedroom? ______.
3. ______ a bed in the bedroom? ______.
4. ______ a chair in the bedroom? ______.

3 **Look.** Write questions.

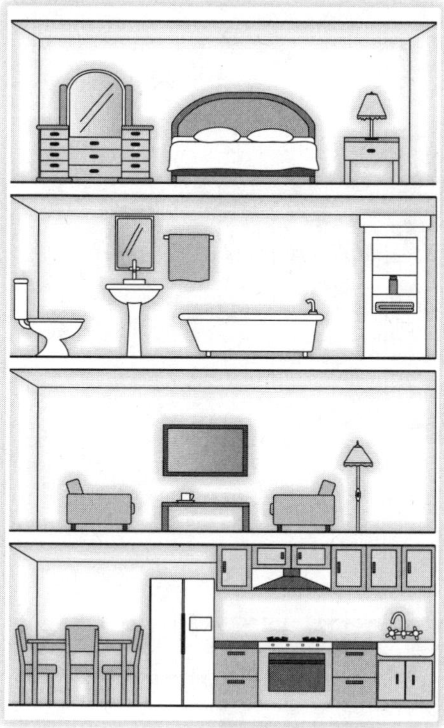

1. Is there a bed in the bedroom?
2. ________________________________?
3. ________________________________?
4. ________________________________?

4 **Write.** Answer your questions from Activity 3.

1. Yes, there is.
2. ________________.
3. ________________.
4. ________________.

5 **Draw and write.** Draw your living room. Write 2 questions and answers.

____

____

____

____

____

Present progressive: *He/She is* + verb-*ing*

Question	Answer
Where is your sister?	She's in the kitchen.

Question			Answer		
What's	she	**doing**?	She's	**eating**.	*What's = What is* *She's = She is*

do → doing   *eat → eating*

1 **Look and read.** Circle the word.

1.  **She / She's** eating.

3.  **He's / He** taking a bath.

2.  She's **sleeping / sleep**.

4.  He's **watching / watch** TV.

2 **Write.** Rewrite the sentences. Use *'s*.

1. He is drawing. He's drawing.
2. She is singing. ________.
3. The baby is sleeping in the bedroom. ________ ________.
4. My brother is watching TV in the living room. ________ ________.

3 Look and write.

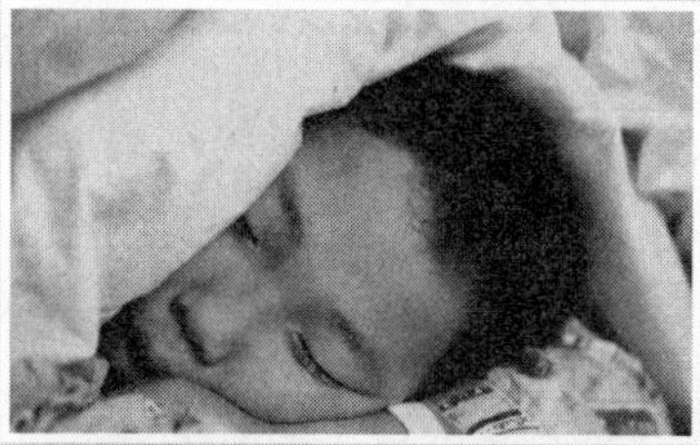

1. Where's your baby sister ?

She's in the bedroom .

She's sleeping .

2. ____________ your mother?

____________________________________.

____________________________________.

3. ____________ your little brother?

____________________________________.

____________________________________.

4. ____________ your sister?

____________________________________.

____________________________________.

4 Draw and write. Draw 2 family members at home. Write.

My father's in the kitchen.

He's cooking.

Unit 5

Present progressive: *am/are/is* + verb-*ing*

Question				Answer			
What	**are**	you	**wearing**?	I'**m**	**wearing**	white shoes.	*I'm = I am*
	is	your brother		He'**s**		a hat.	*He's = He is*
		the girl		She'**s**			*She's = She is*

You can also say:

*My mother'**s wearing** a hat. = My mother **is wearing** a hat.*

*The baby'**s wearing** a hat. = The baby **is wearing** a hat.*

1 Read. Circle.

1. What **is / are** she wearing?
2. What **is / are** you wearing?
3. **She's / She** wearing a red dress.
4. I **'m / 're** wearing gloves.
5. You **'s / 're** wearing socks.
6. I'm **wear / wearing** a skirt.

2 Write. Complete the questions on p. 21.

1. What is your mother wearing?

2. What ________ your brother ____________________?

3. What ________ your father ____________________?

4. What ________ you ____________________?

3 **Color and write.** Use Activity 2.

1. She's wearing green pants.

2. ____________________.

3. ____________________.

4. ____________________.

4 **Look and write.**

1. 

What is he wearing?

He's wearing pants.

He's wearing a shirt.

3. 

____

____

____

____

____

2. 

You

____

____

____

____

____

4. 

____

____

____

____

____

Questions with *that* and *those*

Question		Answer		
What's	**that**?	**That**'s	my pink hat.	*What's = What is*
What are	**those**?	**Those** are	my brown pants.	*That's = That is*

that = one thing

those = two or more things/plurals

1 **Look and read.** Circle the words. Then match.

1.  What's **that / those**? — a. **That / Those** are my gloves.
2.  What are **that / those**? — b. **That's / Those** my hat.
3.  What **'s / are** that? — c. **That's / Those** my skirt.
4.  What **is / are** those? — d. **That's / Those are** my socks.
5.  **What's / What are** that? — e. That **'s / are** my T-shirt.

2 **Write.**

1. What's that ? That's my blue dress.
2. ______________________? Those are my red gloves.
3. ______________________? Those are my black shoes.
4. ______________________? That's my white shirt.
5. ______________________? Those are my brown pants.

3 **Look and write.** Ask and answer questions.

1. What's that ? That's my jacket.

2. ______________? ______________________.

3. ______________? ______________________.

4. ______________? ______________________.

4 **Draw and write.** Draw and color a picture of your clothes. Choose 3 things. Write sentences.

____

____

____

____

Unit 6

Simple present of *want*: *I/you/he, she*

Question				Answer	
Do	you	**want**	a bike?	Yes, I **do**.	*don't* = *do not*
				No, I **don't**. I **want** a train.	
Does	he/she			Yes, he **does**.	*doesn't* = *does not*
				No, she **doesn't**. She **wants** a train.	

To ask a question: ***Do** you + want . . . ?* or ***Does** he/she + want . . . ?*

1 Read. Circle the words.

1. **Do / Does** you want a top? Yes, I **do / does**.
2. **Do / Does** he want a train? Yes, he **do / does**.
3. **Do / Does** she want a bike? Yes, she **does / doesn't**.
4. Do you **want / wants** a ball? No, I **don't / do**.

2 Read and write.

1. Does she want a kite?
2. ________ you want a truck?
3. He ________ a puppet.
4. Does your brother ________ a top?
5. Do you ________ a train?
6. I ________ a bike.

3 **Read and write.** Answer the questions.

1. Do you want a computer? ______________________________.
2. Do you want a big car? ______________________________.
3. Do you want a baby sister? ______________________________.
4. Do you want a bike? ______________________________.

4 **Look and write.**

1. 

   she / 

   Does she want a train ?

   No, she doesn't .

2. 

   he / 

   ______________________________?

   ______________________________.

3. 

   he / 

   ______________________________?

   ______________________________.

4. 

   she / 

   ______________________________?

   ______________________________.

5 **Draw and write.** Draw 2 toys. Ask and answer questions with *want*.

______________________________?

______________________________.

______________________________?

______________________________.

Questions with *this* and *these*

Question		Answer	
Is **this**	your puzzle?	Yes, **it** is.	*isn't = is not*
		No, **it** isn't. **It's** Marco's puzzle.	*It's = It is*
Are **these**	your dolls?	Yes, **they** are.	*aren't = are not*
		No, **they** aren't. **They're** Anita's dolls.	*They're = They are*

For one thing:
*Is **this** your robot? Yes, **it** is.*

For two or more things:
*Are **these** your cars? No, **they** aren't.*

1 Read. Circle the words.

1. Is **this / these** your top?
   No, it **isn't / aren't**.
   It's / They're Juan's top.
2. Are these her **toy / toys**?
   No, they **aren't / isn't**.
   They're / It's my toys.
3. Are **this / these** your balls?
   Yes, **it / they** are.
4. **Are / Is** this your doll?
   No, **it / they** isn't.
   It's her **doll / dolls**.

2 Read and write. Complete the sentences.

1. ____________ your robot?
   Yes, it ____________.
2. ____________ your puzzles?
   No, they ____________. ____________ Bob's puzzles.
3. ____________ her teddy bear?
   No, it ____________.

3 **Look and write.** Ask questions. Follow the model.

1. 
Paolo's
Is this your truck?
____

2. 
Carmen's
____
______________________?

3. 
Maya's
____
______________________?

4. 
Ava's
____
______________________?

4 **Write.** Answer the questions in Activity 3.

1. No, it isn't. It's Paolo's truck.
2. ______________________.
3. ______________________.
4. ______________________.

5 **Write.** Write a conversation between friends about toys. Use the words in the box

aren't	isn't	these	this

____

____

____

____

Review: Units 4–6

1 **Read and match.** Circle the words. Draw a line.

1. What's **that / those**?
2. Is **this / there** a TV in the living room?
3. **Where's / Where** your baby brother?
4. **Is this / Are these** your toy?
5. **Does / Do** she want a doll?

a. He's in the bedroom. He's **sleep / sleeping**.
b. No, she **does / doesn't**.
c. No, **it's / it isn't**.
d. Yes, **there / there is**.
e. **That's / Those are** my game.

2 **Look and write.** Complete the questions and answers.

1. ______________________? That's a photo of my family.
2. Is this your hat? ______________________.
3. What's that? ______________________.
4. ______________________? Yes, I do. I want a chair.
5. ______________________? I'm wearing a shirt.

3 Read and write.

1. Do you want a hat? ☺ ______________________.
2. Do you want brown shoes? ☹ ______________________.
3. ______________________? ☹ ______________________.
   They're my sister's gloves.
4. Does your mother want ______________________? ☺
   ______________________. She wants a computer.

4 **Draw and write.** Draw 2 people in the house. Write about them.

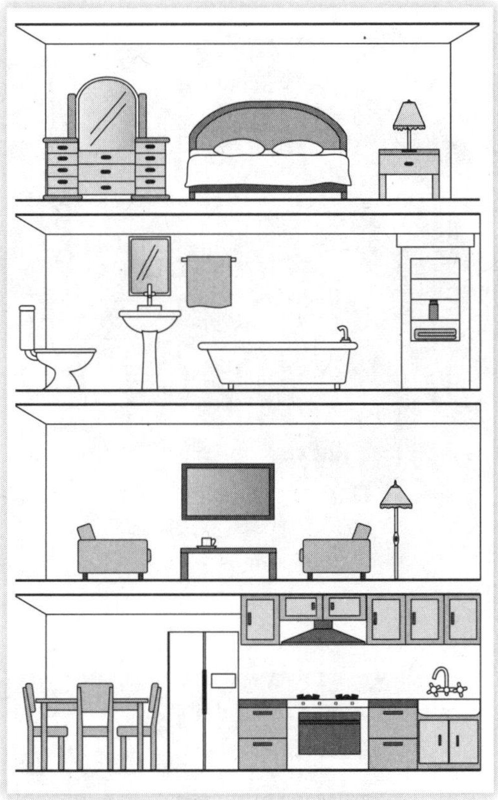

My mother's in the living room.
She's wearing pants and a shirt.
She's watching TV.

5 **Write.** Where are you? What are you wearing? Write sentences.

____

____

Unit 7

Possessive adjectives

I	have	black	hair.	**My**	hair	is	black.
You	have	black	hair.	**Your**	hair	is	black.
He	has	black	hair.	**His**	hair	is	black.
She	has	black	hair.	**Her**	hair	is	black.

The sentences have the same meaning:

I have blue eyes. = ***My*** *eyes are blue.*

1 **Look and read.** Circle the word.

1. **His / Your** hair is black.
2. **His / Their** hair is black.
3. **Her / Their** hair is black.
4. **My / Our** hair is black.
   Your / My eyes are black, too!
5. This is my family.
   Our / Your hair is black.

4 You

2 **Read and write.** Use the words.

1. hair / short Her hair is short.
   eyes / black ______________________.
2. hair / short ______________________.
3. hair / black ______________________.
   eyes / black / too ______________________
   ______________________.

3 **Read.** Rewrite the sentences.

1. I have short hair. My hair is short ______.
2. My father has big ears. ______.
3. You have small hands. ______.
4. My grandmother and grandfather have white hair.

   ______.
5. My little sister has short legs. ______.
6. My baby brother has a small mouth. ______.

4 **Look and write.** Use *her*, *his*, *my*, and *your*.

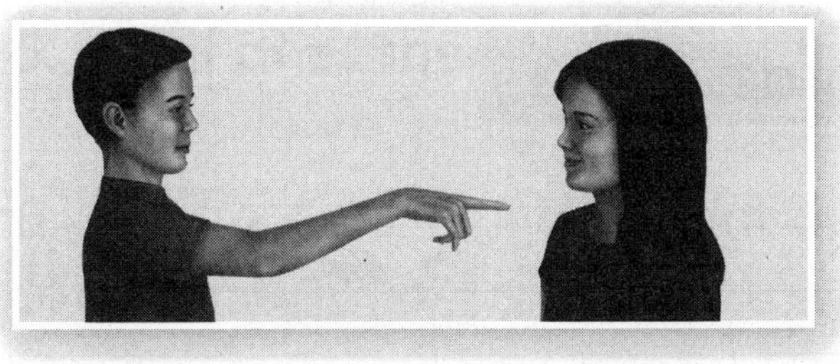

1. ______. (hair) 2. ______. (hand)

   ______. (eyes) ______. (nose)

5 **Write.** Find a photo of friends or family members. Put it here. Write 4 sentences about it.

Put photo here.

______

______

______

______

______

Ability with *can*

I	**can**	draw.
He/She		

Question			Answer	
Can	you	draw?	Yes,	I **can**.
	he/she			he/she **can**.

Use *can* + action word: *I/you/he/she* **can** cook.

1 **Read and match.** Draw a line.

1. I can walk on my hands.
2. I can jump on one foot.
3. She can run and jump.
4. He can walk on his hands, too.

a. He has strong arms.
b. She has strong legs.
c. I have strong arms.
d. I have strong legs.

2 **Write.** Unscramble the words.

1. I / jump / can ______________________________.
2. she / clean / can ______________________________.
3. watch / he / can / TV ______________________________.
4. baby / can / my / sister / eat ______________________________.
5. run / you / can ______________________________?

3 **Look and write.** Write 3 sentences. Use *can*.

She can jump.

____

____

____

4 **Look and write.** Write questions and answers. See p. 9 in your Student's Book.

1. 

Can you draw ____________________?

Yes, I can ____________________.

2. 

____________________?

____________________.

3. 

____________________?

____________________.

4. 

____________________?

____________________.

5 **Write.** Write 4 sentences about your friends or family. Use *can*.

My father can cook.

____

____

____

____

____

Unit 8

like with count and noncount nouns

Question				Answer	
Do	you	**like**	eggs?	Yes, I **do**.	*don't = do not*
				No, I **don't**.	
Does	he		soup?	Yes, he **does**.	*doesn't = does not*
				No, he **doesn't**.	

With *like*, say: *I* ***like*** *apples / bananas / eggs*. (Not: ~~*I like apple/banana/egg*~~.)
I ***like*** *soup*. (Not: ~~*I like soups*~~.)

1 **Read.** Circle your answer.

1. Do you like fish?
   a. Yes, I do. b. No, I don't.
2. Do you like apples?
   a. Yes, I do. b. No, I don't.
3. Do you like chicken?
   a. Yes, I do. b. No, I don't.
4. Do you like rice?
   a. Yes, I do. b. No, I don't.

2 **Read.** Write your answer.

1. Do you like computers? ______________________.
2. Do you like kites? ______________________.
3. Do you like robots? ______________________.
4. Do you like puzzles? ______________________.

3 Read and write.

1. Does he like sandwiches? No, he doesn't. He doesn't like sandwiches.
2. ________ you like oranges? Yes, I ________. I like oranges.
3. Does she ________ cookies? Yes, she does. She ________ cookies.
4. Do you ________ soup? No, I don't. I ________ like soup.
5. ________ she ________ eggs? No, she ________ like eggs.

4 **Read.** Write answers that are true for you.

1. Do you want a cookie? No, I don't. I don't like cookies.
2. Do you want some chicken? ________________________
3. Do you want an apple? ________________________
4. Do you want some rice? ________________________

5 **Look and write.** Write about people in your family.

1.  grandfather Does your grandfather like eggs?
No, he doesn't. He likes chicken.

2.  mother ________________________
____

3.  brother/sister ________________________
____

4.  grandmother ________________________
____

Indefinite articles: *a, an*

a + consonant	banana, cookie, sandwich
an + vowel (a, e, i, o, u)	arm, eraser, orange

Use *a* or *an* with one thing: ***a** banana*, ***a** sandwich*, ***an** eraser*, ***an** orange*.

Don't use *a/an* with these words: *cheese, rice, soup, tea, water, milk, juice.*

1 **Write.** Make 2 lists.

~~apple~~	arm
banana	computer
ear	egg
eraser	fish
mouth	tree

a	an
	apple

2 **Read.** Write *a* or *an*.

1. Is it _____ pencil? No, it isn't. It's _____ table.
2. Is it _____ eraser? Yes, it is!
3. Is there _____ sofa in the living room? No, but there's _____ chair.
4. Does he want _____ apple? No. He wants _____ cookie.
5. There's _____ yellow butterfly. It's not _____ orange butterfly.

3 **Look and write.** Complete the sentences.

1. There is a ___girl___, an ________, a ________, and an ________.
2. There isn't an ________, a ________, a ________, and an ________.

4 Look and write.

1.  an orange

2.  ____________

3.  ____________

4.  ____________

5.  ____________

6.  ____________

7.  ____________

8.  ____________

5 **Write.** Complete the sentences. Use all of the words.

~~board~~	chair	egg	eraser
old toy	~~orange~~	table	umbrella

1. In my classroom, there isn't an orange.

   There is a board.

2. In my living room, there ____________

   ____

3. In my kitchen, there ____________

   ____

4. In my bedroom, there ____________

   ____

Unit 9

Present progressive: *they are* + verb-*ing*

Question				Answer				
	Are	the goats	**running**?	Yes,	they	**are**.		*aren't = are not*
				No,	they	**aren't**.		
What	**are**	they	**doing**?		They**'re**		**eating**.	*They're = They are*

do → doing   eat → eating   run → running

1 Write.

1. sleep They're sleeping.
2. clean ______.
3. walk ______.
4. jump ______.
5. sing ______.
6. eat ______.

2 Read and write.

1. What ______ the cats doing?
2. ______ they running? Yes, they ______.
3. What are the sheep ______?
4. Are ______ jumping? No, they ______.
5. They ______ sleeping.

3 **Look and write.** Use the picture in Activity 2.

1. Are the cows sleeping? ______________________.
2. What are the cats doing? ______________________.
3. Are the goats jumping? ______________________.
4. What are the horses doing? ______________________.
5. Are the goats eating? ______________________.

4 **Look.** Write questions.

1. ______________________? They're eating.
2. ______________________? Yes, they are. They're eating.
3. ______________________? They're walking.
4. ______________________? They're sleeping.
5. ______________________? Yes, they are. They're jumping.

5 **Look and write.** Open your Student's Book to pp. 148–149. Write 3 questions and answers about the picture.

What are the cats doing? They're sleeping.

____

____

____

want + infinitive

Question					Answer	
Do	you	**want**	**to see**	the cows?	Yes, I do.	*don't = do not*
					No, I don't. I **want to see** the ducks.	
Does	Ivan				Yes, he does.	*doesn't = does not*
					No, he doesn't. He **wants to ride** the horse.	

want + *to* + action word: *I **want to feed** the goats. He **wants to see** the chicken.*

1 Read. Circle the answer.

1. Do you **want** / **want to** ride a horse?
2. **Do** / **Does** she want to swim?
3. **Do** / **Does** you want to climb a tree?
4. What **do** / **does** your brother want to do?
5. What **do** / **does** you want to do?
6. What does your father **want** / **wanting** to do?

2 Read and write.

1. I __________ to see the cat.
2. __________ you want to see the cow?
3. What __________ Mei want to do?
4. What does Jian __________ to do?
5. He __________ to see the duck.
6. __________ she want to see the goat? No, she __________.
7. What __________ you __________ to do? I want to see the dog.
8. Do you __________ to see the sheep? No, I __________.

3 **Read.** Write questions.

1. ____________________?
   I want to fly in the sky.
2. ____________________?
   She wants to ride a bike.
3. ____________________?
   She wants to crawl on the grass.
4. ____________________?
   No, he doesn't. My father wants to read.
5. ____________________?
   No, I don't. I don't like cats.

4 **Write.** Write questions.

~~in your kitchen~~ in your living room
at school with your friends with your parents

1. What do you want to do in your kitchen?
2. ____________________?
3. ____________________?
4. ____________________?
5. ____________________?

5 **Read and write.** Answer the questions in Activity 4.

1. I want to cook.
2. ____________________.
3. ____________________.
4. ____________________.
5. ____________________.

Review: Units 7–9

1 Read and match. Circle the words. Then draw a line.

1. Do you **like / likes** turtles?
2. What are the sheep **do / doing**?
3. **Is / Are** the dogs sleeping?
4. What does Eve **want / wants** to do?
5. **Does / Do** he like cats?

a. They **'re / 's** running.
b. She **want / wants** to cook.
c. Yes, he **do / does**.
d. No, they **are / aren't**.
e. Yes, I **do / does**.

2 Look and write.

1. 
an apple

2. 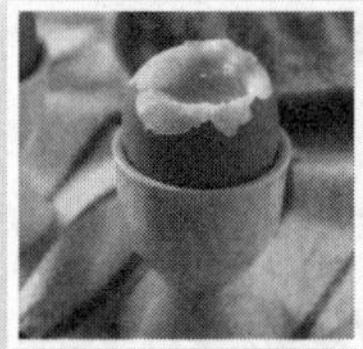
____

3. 
____

4. 
____

5. 
____

6. 
____

3 Look and write. What can they do?

1. ________________.
2. ________________.
3. ________________.
4. ________________.

4 **Look and write.** Use the picture from Activity 3.

1. What color is the girl's hair? ______________________.
2. What color are the boy's pants? ______________________.
3. What are the sheep doing? ______________________.
4. What does the girl want to do? ______________________.
5. Does the boy like climbing? ______________________.

5 **Read.** Write questions.

1. ______________________?

   Yes, I do. I like soup very much.

2. ______________________?

   They're jumping.

3. ______________________?

   My mother wants to clean.

4. ______________________?

   No, they aren't cooking. They're eating.

5. ______________________?

   No, I don't. I don't want to run.

6 **Write.** Write about you. Use *can*, *like*, and *want*.

____

____

____

____

Review: Units 1–9

1 Read. Circle.

1. **a** / **an** apple
2. **a** / **an** sheep
3. **a** / **an** top
4. **a** / **an** eye
5. **a** / **an** arm
6. **a** / **an** eraser

2 Read and write.

1. My mother's hair is brown. Her hair is brown ______.
2. My grandfather's gloves are red. ______.
3. I have a truck. It's orange. ______.
4. You have a pencil. It's green. ______.

3 Look and write.

1. Who's she? ______
______.
2. What is it? ______.
3. ______?
Yes, it is.
4. What's that? ______.
5. Where is the top? ______
______.
6. ______? No, it isn't. It's my sister's train.
7. ______? I'm wearing a shirt.

4 Read and write.

1. Does your brother want a cat?  ____________________.
2. Is this Dana's doll?  ____________________.
3. Are these our toys?  ____________________.
4. Do you want to eat chicken?  ____________________.

5 Read and write.

1. Do you want crayons? ____________________.
2. Do you like milk? ____________________.
3. Do you want to ride a horse? ____________________.
4. What are you wearing? ____________________.
5. How many grandmothers do you have? ____________________.

6 Read and write. Ask questions.

1. ____________________? That's my bike.
2. ____________________? No, he doesn't want a cookie.
3. ____________________? Yes, I do. I like turtles.
4. ____________________? Yes, I do. I want a computer.
5. ____________________? He's in the kitchen. He's cooking.
6. ____________________? I have two books.
7. ____________________? He's my brother.

7 **Look and write.** Use the words.

1. What color is the bird ________? (color)

   It's white ________. (white)

2. ________? (it)

   ________. (river)

3. ________? (many)

   ________. (three)

4. ________? (doing)

   ________. (jumping)

8 **Write.** Write 4 sentences about you. Use the words in the box.

can	like	my	want (to)	wearing

____

____

____

____

GAME

Read and write. Complete the sentences. Match letters and shapes.

1. ___ ___ ___ is she? ___ ___ ___ is my ___ ___ ___ ___ sister.

2. Is ___ ___ ___ ___ ___ a ___ ___ ___ ___ in the bedroom?

   Yes, there is. The lamp is next to the bed.

3. Do you want a pen? ___ ___ ___, I do.

4. ___ ___ ___ these ___ ___ ___ ___ shoes? Yes, they are my shoes.

5. What does she ___ ___ ___ ___ to do? She wants to sleep.

6. ___ ___ ___ ___ she want a cat? ___ ___, she doesn't.

7. It's hot. Take ___ ___ ___ your ___ ___ ___ ___ ___ ___.

8. Where's your ___ ___ ___ ___ ___ ___ ___ ___ ___ ___ ___?

   He's in the kitchen with my father and brother. He ___ ___ cooking.

9. ___ ___ it a ___ ___ ___ ___ ___? Yes, it is a horse.

Mystery message: